Mykonos Travel guide 2023

From Budget to Luxury: A step by-step guide to a stress free travel experience in Mykonos, Greece.

Robert Carpenter

Table of content

Introduction

Mykonos, which is one of the most stunning and well-liked tourist attractions in Greece, lies tucked away in the middle of the Aegean Sea. Mykonos is a must-see for anybody visiting Greece because of its breathtaking beaches, beautiful ocean, and exciting nightlife. Mykonos offers a variety of holiday options, including family-friendly activities, crazy parties, and romantic getaways.

I chose to take my family on a vacation to Mykonos. Elizabeth, my wife, and my boys, Peter and Stephen. I have a busy and frantic life in the city with my wife Elizabeth. We decided to book a vacation to the stunning Greek island of Mykonos since we were in desperate need of a break from the chaos.

The moment we got off the boat on the day of our visit, we were awestruck by the island's charm and beauty. They had never seen anything like the white-washed structures, blue-domed cathedrals, and windmills before.

The first place my family went was to a beautiful beach in the south of the island, where we sat in the sun all day, played in the clear water, and made sand castles. My wife was happy to have some downtime since the kids were in paradise.

We decided to see the town the next day. We took a stroll through the congested, twisting alleys, pausing to take in the distinctive Cycladic architecture and stopping at quaint boutiques and tavernas. We had a great local meal that evening, which included grilled octopus and tzatziki, and we finished the day with a stunning sunset from Little Venice.

We continued our exploration of the island over the next few days, stopping at more gorgeous beaches such as Super Paradise

Beach and Elia Beach as well as taking a picturesque boat cruise to the adjacent islet of Delos. We also experimented with novel sports like kayaking and snorkeling, exploring the breathtaking underwater environment of the island.

Chapter 1

History

Mykonos is a beautiful Greek island located in the Aegean Sea that has a rich and fascinating history dating back thousands of years. Archaeological evidence suggests that the island was inhabited as early as the 3rd millennium BCE and was a significant center for trade and commerce in ancient times.

In the 8th century BCE, Mykonos became an important religious center for the worship of the god Apollo. The island was said to be the birthplace of Hercules and was also known for the famous Battle of Mykonos, where Hercules defeated the Giants. The island was also home to several important sanctuaries dedicated to Apollo and other gods and goddesses.

During the Hellenistic period, Mykonos became a thriving center of trade and commerce, with a bustling port and a thriving economy. The island was famous for its production of wine and olive oil, which were exported to other parts of the Aegean and beyond.

In the 4th century BCE, Mykonos was conquered by the Romans and became part of the Roman Empire. During this time, the island continued to thrive as a center of trade and commerce, and was known for its prosperity and wealth.

In the Middle Ages, Mykonos was invaded by the Venetians, who established a strong presence on the island. The island was also occupied by the Ottoman Turks for many years and was finally incorporated into the newly independent Greek state in the 19th century.

In the 20th century, Mykonos underwent a significant transformation, becoming a popular tourist destination and a center of the international jet set. The island's stunning beaches, crystal-clear waters, and vibrant nightlife attracted travelers from all over the world, and it became one of the most famous and popular tourist destinations in Greece.

Today, Mykonos continues to be a popular holiday destination, attracting millions of visitors each year. The island is famous for its charming traditional architecture, its stunning beaches, its delicious local cuisine, and its legendary nightlife. Mykonos is a unique and fascinating place that embodies the spirit of Greece and has a rich and diverse history that has shaped its unique character and identity.

Chapter 2

Best time to visit, weather, and safety on the island

Mykonos is a popular tourist destination known for its stunning beaches, vibrant nightlife, and charming architecture. Whether you're looking to soak up the sun, party the night away, or simply relax and enjoy the scenery, Mykonos has something for everyone. However, the best time to visit Mykonos depends on a number of factors, including personal preferences, budget, and what you hope to experience while you're there.

May to June and September to October are considered the best months to visit Mykonos. During these months, the weather is warm and sunny, the crowds are smaller, and prices are lower compared to peak summer season. The sea is also calm and perfect for swimming, snorkeling, and other water activities.

In the summer months of July and August, Mykonos is at its busiest. The island is packed with tourists, the beaches are crowded, and the prices are at their highest. However, this is also the best time to experience Mykonos' famous nightlife, with parties and events happening all over the island. If you're looking for a more lively and energetic experience, summer may be the best time for you to visit.

The shoulder seasons of spring and fall can also be a great time to visit Mykonos. The weather is still warm and pleasant, and the crowds are smaller. However, some of the island's popular attractions and beaches may not be fully operational during these times, so it's important to check ahead before planning your trip.

In terms of cost, the summer months are generally the most expensive, while the shoulder seasons offer more budget-friendly options. If you're traveling on a tight budget, it's best to avoid visiting Mykonos in July and August, as prices for accommodations, food, and activities are significantly higher during these months.

No matter when you visit Mykonos, it's important to be prepared for the island's strong winds and hot sun. Pack light, airy clothing, sunscreen, and a hat to protect yourself from the elements. It's also a good idea to bring comfortable walking shoes, as many of the island's attractions are best explored on foot.

In summary, the best time to visit Mykonos depends on your personal preferences and what you hope to experience while you're there.

Chapter 3

Weather on Mykonos Island

Mykonos has a Mediterranean climate with scorching summers and moderate winters. The island regularly sees high temperatures from June through September, with temperatures ranging from 80-90°F. The months of July and August are considered the peak season, with high humidity and minimal rainfall. Despite the heat, the island's powerful winds, known as the "Meltemi", give respite from the heat and also bring cold sea breezes to the shore. During the winter months, temperatures are substantially milder, with temps ranging from 50-60°F.

Safety Precautions

Sun Safety: With the scorching temperatures on Mykonos, it's crucial to protect your skin from damaging UV radiation. Wear a hat, sunglasses, and apply sunscreen periodically.

Hydration: It's easy to get dehydrated in the hot weather, so be sure to drink lots of water and remain hydrated.

Water Safety: Mykonos has several gorgeous beaches, but it's vital to take care while swimming in the water. Always swim in approved places and never swim alone. If you're unclear about the conditions, contact a lifeguard for guidance.

Wind Safety: The high winds on the island may make outdoor activities tough, so be cautious to hang onto your hat and secure any loose things. The winds may also make sea conditions harsh, so be careful while boating or engaging in water sports.

Travel Safety: When touring the island, be mindful of your surroundings and take the essential steps to remain safe. Avoid going alone at night and keep expensive goods protected.

Health Safety: If you're going from a foreign country, be careful to consult with your doctor about any required vaccines or health precautions. In case of sickness or injury, seek medical treatment soon.

Chapter 4

Essential travel advice to mykonos

To minimize disappointment, plan your vacation ahead of time and schedule your lodgings, activities, and transportation.

Pack light, bearing in mind the Mediterranean temperature and the laid-back, informal character of the island.

To move about effectively, familiarize yourself with the island's geography and transportation alternatives, including buses and taxis.

To avoid crowds and save money, try to skip peak season, which is July and August.

Respect the island's relaxed pace by spending a few hours each day resting and taking up the sun and environment.

Spend a day or two touring the adjacent islands after taking advantage of Mykonos' beaches, which are among the finest in Greece.

Fresh fish, classic Greek foods, and the famed Mykonian loukoumades are among the local delicacies.

Keep valuables and critical papers secure, and be wary of pickpockets, particularly in popular tourist areas.

As Mykonos is a major tourist destination, it is important to protect its natural beauty. Be conscious of your environmental effect and properly dispose of your rubbish.

Finally, be open to new experiences, experiment with new things, and respect the local culture and people.

Chapter 5

25 key facts to know about Mykonos before you visit

- Mykonos is a Greek island in the Aegean Sea, part of the Cyclades island group.

- It is a popular tourist destination known for its vibrant nightlife, beautiful beaches, and whitewashed architecture.

- The island's main town, also called Mykonos, is known for its charming, narrow streets and iconic windmills.

- The island's most famous beach, Paradise Beach, is a popular spot for partying and sunbathing.

- Mykonos is also home to several other picturesque beaches, such as Super Paradise Beach and Elia Beach.

- The island is famous for its traditional Cycladic architecture, with houses and buildings painted in white and blue.

- Mykonos has a rich cultural heritage, with several historic churches, including the 16th-century Panagia Paraportiani.

- The island has a Mediterranean climate, with hot summers and mild winters.

- Mykonos is known for its active nightlife, with numerous clubs, bars, and restaurants open until the early hours of the morning.

- The island also has a thriving food scene, with traditional Greek cuisine and international dining options.

- Mykonos is connected to the mainland and other islands by ferry services, as well as by air via its airport.

- The island has a number of luxury resorts and boutique hotels, as well as more budget-friendly accommodation options.

- Mykonos is a popular destination for LGBTQ+ travelers, with a lively gay scene.

- The island is also popular with celebrities and high-end travelers, with several exclusive beach clubs and restaurants.

- The island has a long history, dating back to ancient times, and has been inhabited by various civilizations over the centuries.

- Mykonos has a unique geological formation, with its rocky coastline, rolling hills, and numerous coves and bays.

- The island is surrounded by crystal-clear waters, making it a popular spot for swimming, snorkeling, and diving.

- There are several opportunities for outdoor activities on Mykonos, such as hiking, horseback riding, and windsurfing.

- The island is also home to several historic landmarks and museums, including the Archaeological Museum of Mykonos and the Aegean Maritime Museum.

- The island is famous for its traditional festivals, such as the Mykonos International Film Festival and the Mykonos Blues Festival.

- Mykonos has a thriving local arts scene, with several galleries and workshops showcasing the work of local artists.

- The island is also known for its unique shopping scene, with everything from souvenir shops to high-end boutiques.

- Mykonos is a popular destination for yachting, with several marinas and yacht clubs located on the island.

- The island is home to several scenic villages, such as Ano Mera, which is known for its traditional architecture and tranquil atmosphere.

- Mykonos is known for its legendary hospitality and friendly local community, making it a welcoming destination for visitors.

Chapter 6

10 Do's and Don'ts for first time tourist to Mykonos

Do's:

Pack appropriately for the weather:
It is important to pack appropriately for the weather at your destination. This includes researching the climate and weather conditions, as well as considering the activities you have planned. Pack clothes that are suitable for the weather, such as lightweight, breathable clothes for hot weather, and warm, waterproof clothing for cooler weather. Don't forget to also pack items such as sunglasses, a hat, sunscreen, and a rain jacket if necessary. Packing appropriately for the weather can help ensure that you stay comfortable and safe during your trip.

Try local food and drink:

Definitely! Trying local food and drink is a great way to immerse yourself in the local culture and get a taste of the destination. You can try traditional dishes and drinks, visit local markets like the chora local market which is located in the main town of mykonos, selling everything from souvenirs and handmade crafts to fresh produce and spices, or explore local restaurants and cafes. This can be a great way to experience the local cuisine and learn about the culture and history of the area. When trying local food and drink, it is important to be mindful of any dietary restrictions or allergies you may have.

Respect the local culture and customs:

Yes, it is important to respect the local culture and customs when traveling. This includes being mindful of local traditions, customs, and laws, as well as being aware of local attitudes and values. Some ways to show respect include dressing appropriately, being polite and courteous, and avoiding behavior that may be considered offensive or inappropriate.

Additionally, it is important to be respectful of local wildlife and natural resources, as well as taking steps to reduce your environmental impact. By respecting the local culture and customs, you can have a more positive and enjoyable travel experience, as well as contributing to the preservation of the local culture for future generations.

Get travel insurance:

It is highly recommended to get travel insurance before embarking on your trip. Travel insurance can provide coverage for unexpected events such as medical emergencies, trip cancellations, flight delays, and lost or stolen luggage. Having travel insurance can give you peace of mind and financial protection during your trip, allowing you to focus on enjoying your

Travel experience: When choosing a travel insurance policy, it is important to consider the specific coverage you need, such as medical coverage, trip cancellations, and emergency evacuation. It is also important to review the policy carefully to understand the terms and conditions, as well as any exclusions or limitations.

Plan your transportation in advance:
It is a good idea to plan your transportation in advance when traveling to Mykonos. This can help ensure that you have a smooth and efficient trip, and avoid any unnecessary stress or inconvenience. Depending on your travel plans, you may need to arrange transportation from the airport, or between different destinations on the island. Some options for transportation in Mykonos include taxis, buses, car rentals, or private transfers. You can also consider using local ferries or water taxis to explore the nearby islands. By planning your transportation in advance, you can ensure that you have a

reliable and convenient way to get around during your trip.

Stay safe and take basic precautions:
It is important to stay safe and take basic precautions when traveling to Mykonos. Here are some tips for staying safe:

Be aware of your surroundings and take note of emergency exits in public places:
Avoid walking alone at night in unfamiliar areas.

Keep your valuables, passport, and money in a safe and secure place.

Use ATMs in well-lit and secure areas.

Be cautious of pickpockets and keep an eye on your belongings.

Always carry a fully charged phone and let someone know your plans and whereabouts.

Avoid overindulging in alcohol and drugs.

Know the local emergency numbers and how to contact the police, ambulance, and fire services.

Avoid revealing sensitive or personal information to strangers.

Familiarize yourself with local customs and laws, and respect them.
By following these basic precautions and being aware of your personal safety, you can have a safe and enjoyable trip to Mykonos.

Take advantage of the local tourism industry:
Taking advantage of the local tourism industry in Mykonos can enhance your travel experience. There are many ways to do this, including:

Booking tours and excursions: There are many local tour companies that offer guided tours and excursions to popular tourist attractions and landmarks. This can be a great way to learn about the history, culture, and natural beauty of Mykonos.

Experiencing local events and festivals: Mykonos is known for its vibrant cultural scene and hosts many events and festivals throughout the year. From music and dance festivals to traditional celebrations, these events offer a unique opportunity to immerse yourself in local culture.

Supporting local businesses: When shopping, dining, or booking accommodations, consider supporting local businesses. This can help stimulate the local economy and promote sustainable tourism.

Learning about local history and culture: There are many museums and cultural centers in Mykonos that showcase the rich history and cultural heritage of the island. Visiting these sites can provide insight into the local way of life and help you understand the significance of the place.

By taking advantage of the local tourism industry in Mykonos, you can have a more meaningful and memorable travel experience.

Have a backup plan in case of emergency: It is always a good idea to have a backup plan in case of an emergency while traveling. This can help you stay safe and prepared in the event of unexpected events, such as natural disasters, medical emergencies, or other unpredictable situations.

Some steps you can take to prepare for emergencies include:

Research local emergency services and medical facilities before your trip.

Store important information, such as your passport, travel insurance policy, and emergency contact numbers, in a safe and accessible place.

Keep a list of local emergency services and their contact information in your phone or carry a printed copy with you.

Consider carrying a small first-aid kit and any necessary medications.

Make sure someone back home has a copy of your itinerary and emergency contact information.

Stay informed of local weather conditions and be prepared to adjust your plans if necessary.

By having a backup plan in case of emergency, you can be better prepared to handle unexpected events and minimize any potential risks during your trip to Mykonos.

Stay hydrated and eat regularly: Staying hydrated and eating regularly are important for maintaining your health and well-being while traveling in Mykonos. Here are some tips for staying hydrated and nourished during your trip:

Drink plenty of water: Dehydration is a common issue for travelers, especially during hot summer months in Mykonos. Make sure to drink enough water throughout the day to stay hydrated.

Eat regularly: Skipping meals or going long periods without eating can lead to fatigue and low energy levels. Make sure to eat a balanced diet that includes a variety of fruits, vegetables, and whole grains.

Try local cuisine: Mykonos is known for its delicious food and dining options, including fresh seafood and traditional Greek dishes. Don't miss the opportunity to try some of the local specialties.

Avoid street food if you have any food sensitivities: Street food can be tempting, but it can also be a source of food-borne illnesses for some travelers. If you have any food sensitivities, consider eating at established restaurants or cafes.

Keep snacks on hand: Pack some healthy snacks, such as fruit, granola bars, or nuts, to keep you fueled during your travels.

By staying hydrated and eating regularly, you can help ensure that you have the energy and stamina to fully enjoy your travel experience in Mykonos

Take lots of photos and memories: Mykonos is known for its picturesque landscapes and charming architecture, making it a great destination for taking memorable photos. Some of the most amazing places in Mykonos to take photos are:

Little Venice: A neighborhood with charming traditional buildings and a sea-front promenade, perfect for capturing the iconic Mykonian sunset.

Paradise Beach: A famous party beach with crystal clear waters and stunning views, ideal for beach and landscape shots.

The Windmills of Mykonos: A row of iconic windmills that have become a symbol of the island, perfect for capturing the essence of Mykonos.

Mykonos Town (Chora): The main town is filled with narrow winding streets, traditional white-washed buildings, and colorful doors and windows, great for street photography.

The Archaeological Museum of Mykonos: A stunning museum that showcases ancient artifacts and exhibits, perfect for architecture and history enthusiasts.

The Church of Paraportiani: A famous Mykonian church made of four separate structures, great for architectural photography.

These are just a few of the many photo-worthy places in Mykonos, and you'll surely find many more memorable spots to capture during your visit.

Don'ts:

Don't overspend: Here are some tips to help you avoid overspending while on vacation in Mykonos:

Plan your budget and stick to it: Decide on a daily or overall budget for your trip and try to stick to it as closely as possible.

Choose affordable accommodations: Look for accommodations that fit your budget and location preferences, such as a budget-friendly hotel or a rental apartment.

Be mindful of food and drinks expenses: Eat at local taverns and cafes, which are often more affordable than tourist-oriented restaurants. Consider buying groceries and cooking some of your meals to save money.

These are some of the amazing restaurants I and my family visited while having a nice time on the island. Avra Taverna - a traditional Greek restaurant with a focus on fresh, locally-sourced ingredients

Nikolas Taverna - a family-run spot serving up classic Greek dishes

Kiki's Taverna - a popular restaurant known for its delicious fresh fish and friendly service

Kaizer's - a cozy taverna offering a variety of dishes, from meze platters to grilled meats

Peskesi - a contemporary taverna serving up modern Greek cuisine with a focus on organic ingredients

These are just a few options to consider, and of course prices and options may change over time.

Avoid overpriced tourist traps:
Research the island ahead of time and avoid visiting overpriced tourist attractions and shops. Instead, find free or low-cost activities such as visiting the beaches, hiking, or exploring the town.

Use public transportation: Taxis and rental cars can be expensive in Mykonos. Consider using public transportation, such as the bus, to save money on transportation costs.

By following these tips, you can have a wonderful vacation in Mykonos without breaking the bank.

Don't ignore local laws and regulations:
To avoid ignoring local laws and regulations in Mykonos, you should familiarize yourself with the local laws and regulations and make sure to comply with them while you

are there. This may include respecting noise ordinances, following traffic laws, and avoiding activities that are illegal, such as drug use. Additionally, it's important to be respectful of the local culture and customs. Don't neglect to plan for safety and security. Here are some tips to ensure safety and security while traveling to Mykonos:

Research the local area and stay informed of any safety or security concerns.

Make copies of important documents (passport, ID, etc.) and store them in a secure location.

Use a money belt or hidden pouch to store your valuables and keep them close to your body at all times.

Be cautious of pickpockets, especially in crowded areas.

Avoid walking alone at night and be aware of your surroundings at all times.

Follow local laws and customs, especially regarding drug and alcohol use.

Make sure your travel insurance covers any activities you plan to undertake.

Store the contact information for the local embassy and emergency services in your phone.

Stay in touch with family and friends, especially if you are traveling alone.

Don't carry large amounts of cash:
it's recommended not to carry large amounts of cash while traveling to Mykonos. Instead, consider using credit or debit cards and only withdraw the cash you need for the day. Make sure to only use ATMs located in secure, well-lit areas, and keep an eye out for signs of skimming devices. Additionally,

consider using a travel money card that can be easily canceled if lost or stolen. This way, you can keep your funds safe and secure while enjoying your vacation.

Don't ignore the advice of locals or travel professionals.

By following these tips, you can ensure that you make the most of your vacation in Mykonos and have a memorable and enriching experience.

Be open-minded: Be open to new experiences and suggestions from locals and professionals. They have lived and worked in the area for a long time and have valuable insights and tips to share.

Ask for recommendations: Ask locals and professionals for recommendations on things to do, see, and eat. They can give you an insider's perspective on the best places to visit.

Listen and observe: Pay attention to the locals and take note of the things they do. This will give you a better understanding of their culture and way of life.

Respect local customs: Respect local customs and traditions. This will help you avoid offending anyone and will enhance your overall experience.

Show appreciation: Thank locals and professionals for their help and advice. A small gesture of appreciation can go a long way in building positive relationships.

Don't assume everything will be like it is at home:
It is always a good idea to be aware of cultural differences and local customs when traveling to a new place, even if Mykonos is a popular tourist destination. This can help ensure that you have a positive and respectful experience during your vacation.

Some things to consider may include differences in language, currency, food, customs, and laws. Keep an open mind and be willing to embrace new experiences, but also be prepared to adapt to the local environment.

Don't ignore health and safety warnings: It is important to take health and safety warnings seriously while on vacation in Mykonos. This may include following local health guidelines, such as, practicing good hygiene, and being aware of potential safety hazards. Additionally, it is important to familiarize yourself with local emergency procedures and to have travel insurance in case of unexpected events.

Don't forget to bring important documents:

It is important to remember to bring important documents such as a passport, visa (if required), driver's license, and any other relevant identification. It is also a good idea to make copies or have electronic versions of these documents in case of loss or theft.

Don't neglect to bring adequate travel insurance:

Travel insurance is important to have when traveling as it provides coverage for unexpected events such as trip cancellations, medical emergencies, and lost or stolen luggage. It is important to choose a travel insurance policy that fits your specific needs and provides adequate coverage. Before purchasing a travel insurance policy, it is a good idea to research and compare different options, read the policy terms and conditions, and understand what is covered and what is not covered.

Don't forget to bring appropriate clothing and supplies:

It is important to bring appropriate clothing and supplies while traveling to Mykonos. Some recommended items include:

Light, comfortable clothing and footwear for the hot weather
Swimwear for the beaches
Sun protection such as hats, sunglasses, and sunblock
Cash and credit cards
First aid kit
Camera for capturing memories
Adaptors for electronics if necessary
A refillable water bottle
Remember to also check the weather forecast and pack accordingly.

Chapter 7

Visas and travel documents

In order to enter Greece, including Mykonos, travelers need to have the appropriate visa and travel documents. The specific requirements depend on the traveler's nationality, length of stay, and purpose of visit.

European Union (EU) and European Economic Area (EEA) citizens:
Citizens of EU and EEA countries, as well as Switzerland, are free to enter Greece without a visa for stays of up to 90 days. They only need to present a valid passport or national ID card.

Visa-exempt non-EU citizens:
Citizens of some countries, such as the United States, Australia, Canada, and New Zealand, are also allowed to enter Greece without a visa for stays of up to 90 days.

However, it's always best to check the specific visa requirements for your country before traveling to Greece.

Visa-required non-EU citizens:
Citizens of some countries need a visa to enter Greece, depending on the length of their stay and the purpose of their visit. For example, travelers who are visiting Greece for business purposes or to study may need a different visa than those who are traveling for tourism.

Travel documents for minors:
Minors (children under the age of 18) traveling to Greece must have a valid passport or national ID card, if applicable. Minors traveling with one parent or without a parent should carry a notarized letter of consent from the absent parent(s).
it's essential to check the specific visa requirements for your country before traveling to Mykonos, Greece. By having the

appropriate visa and travel documents, you can ensure a smooth and hassle-free trip.
Getting A Greek visa upon Arrival

If you are a citizen of a country that requires a visa to enter Greece, you may have the option to obtain a Greek visa upon arrival. This means that you can apply for and receive your visa at the airport or port of entry in Greece, rather than applying for it in advance at a Greek embassy or consulate. In this chapter, we'll provide a comprehensive guide on how to get a Greek visa upon arrival.

Eligibility:
Not all travelers are eligible to obtain a Greek visa upon arrival. This option is generally only available to travelers who are visiting Greece for short-term purposes, such as tourism, business, or transit. If you are planning to stay in Greece for more than 90 days, you will need to apply for a

long-term visa in advance, as the visa upon arrival is only valid for short-term stays.

Requirements:

To obtain a Greek visa upon arrival, you will need to meet certain requirements. These requirements may vary depending on your country of origin, but generally, you will need to have a valid passport, proof of financial support for your stay in Greece, and a return ticket or proof of onward travel. It's important to check the specific requirements for your country before traveling to Greece.

Visa fee:

There is a fee for obtaining a Greek visa upon arrival, which is typically around 60 euros. The fee may vary depending on the type of visa you are applying for and your country of origin. You will need to pay the visa fee in cash, as credit and debit cards are not accepted.

Application process:
To apply for a Greek visa upon arrival, you will need to go to the visa office at the airport or port of entry in Greece. There, you will need to complete an application form and provide the necessary documents, such as your passport and proof of financial support. You will also need to pay the visa fee.

Wait time:
The wait time for processing your Greek visa upon arrival may vary, but it's usually between 30 minutes and several hours, depending on the number of applicants and the time of day. It's important to be patient and allow enough time for the visa processing, as missing your flight or onward travel plans due to a long wait time can be stressful and costly.

Chapter 8

Visa extension

If you plan to stay in Greece for more than 90 days, you will need to apply for a long-term visa, such as a student visa or a work visa. The application process and requirements for these visas vary, so it's important to check with the Greek embassy or consulate in your home country for more information.

The popular tourist destination in Greece attracts thousands of visitors every year. While most visitors come to Mykonos on a short-term tourist visa, some may wish to extend their stay. In this chapter, we will discuss the process of visa extension in Mykonos, Greece.

Who is Eligible for a Visa Extension in Mykonos?

Visitors who have entered Greece on a short-term tourist visa (C-Type visa) are eligible to apply for a visa extension. However, there are some restrictions on who can apply for a visa extension, such as those who have overstayed their visa, those with a criminal record, or those who pose a security threat to Greece.

How to Apply for a Visa Extension in Mykonos

To apply for a visa extension, visitors must first ensure that they meet the eligibility requirements. If they do, they must follow the following steps:

Gather required documents: Visitors must prepare and gather the necessary documents for the visa extension application, including a valid passport, two passport-sized photographs, proof of sufficient funds for their stay, and proof of medical insurance.

Submit the application: Visitors must submit their visa extension application at the local police station in Mykonos. The police station will stamp the application and forward it to the Ministry of Citizen Protection in Athens for review.

Wait for the decision: After submitting the application, visitors must wait for the decision on their visa extension. This can take several weeks or even months. Visitors should check the status of their application regularly and be prepared to provide additional information or documents if required.

Receive the visa: If the visa extension is approved, visitors will receive the visa and must pay the fee. They will then be able to continue their stay in Greece for the length of the extension.

The timeframe for a visa extension in Mykonos can vary depending on the individual circumstances and the workload of the Ministry of Citizen Protection. On average, the process can take several weeks or even months. Visitors are advised to apply for a visa extension well in advance of the expiration of their current visa.

Fees for a Visa Extension in Mykonos

Visitors must pay a fee for a visa extension in Mykonos. The fee can vary depending on the length of the extension and other factors, such as the number of entries allowed. Visitors must pay the fee in person at the local police station after the visa extension has been approved.

Chapter 9

Budgeting and cost considerations

Mykonos, known for its beautiful beaches, vibrant nightlife, and picturesque architecture, is a popular vacation destination for travelers from around the world. While a vacation in Mykonos can be an unforgettable experience, it's important to be mindful of budgeting and cost factors. In this chapter, we'll provide a comprehensive guide on budgeting and cost factors for a vacation in Mykonos.

Accommodation:

Accommodation is one of the biggest costs for a vacation in Mykonos, and prices can vary greatly depending on the type of accommodation you choose. For budget-friendly options, you can opt for a basic hotel room or a hostel, while more luxurious options include villas, resorts, and five-star hotels. The cost of accommodation in Mykonos is higher during the peak tourist season, which runs from June to September, so it's best to book early if you're traveling during this time.

Food and drinks:
Food and drinks in Mykonos can also be expensive, especially in tourist areas. A meal in a restaurant can range from 20-30 euros per person, while a drink in a bar or club can cost between 10-15 euros. To save money on food, you can opt for street food, local tavernas, or supermarkets to purchase groceries and prepare your own meals.

Transportation:
Getting around Mykonos can be expensive, as taxis and rental cars are the main modes of transportation. A taxi ride can cost between 15-20 euros, while a rental car can cost around 50-70 euros per day. To save money on transportation, you can opt for public buses, which are more affordable, or

rent a scooter or bicycle to explore the island.

Activities and attractions:
The cost of activities and attractions in Mykonos can vary greatly depending on what you choose to do. A visit to one of the island's famous beaches can be free, while more structured activities such as boat tours, water sports, or archaeological sites can cost between 20-50 euros per person. It's best to research the cost of activities and attractions in advance to better plan your budget.

Shopping:
Mykonos is known for its shopping, with a variety of boutiques, shops, and markets selling local products and souvenirs. The cost of shopping in Mykonos can vary, but it's best to budget at least 50-100 euros for souvenirs and gifts.

Miscellaneous expenses:
There are other miscellaneous expenses to consider when budgeting for a vacation in Mykonos, such as travel insurance, visas (if applicable), and tipping. It's best to budget an additional 10-15% of the overall cost of your trip for these miscellaneous expenses.

In conclusion, budgeting and cost factors are important considerations for a vacation in Mykonos. The main costs are typically accommodation, food and drinks, transportation, activities and attractions, shopping, and miscellaneous expenses. It's best to research the cost of each expense in advance and budget accordingly to ensure a stress-free and enjoyable vacation in Mykonos.

Chapter 10

Must see landmarks and attractions

In this chapter, we'll provide a comprehensive guide on must-see landmarks and attractions for a vacation in Mykonos.

Little Venice:

Little Venice is one of the most picturesque neighborhoods in Mykonos, famous for its colorful buildings and stunning sea views. The area is located along the coast and is home to some of the island's most popular bars and restaurants. Visitors can take a leisurely stroll along the promenade and enjoy the views of the Aegean Sea, making it a must-see attraction for any traveler to Mykonos.

Mykonos Windmills:

The Mykonos Windmills are a famous landmark on the island and are an iconic symbol of Mykonos. The windmills, which were used for milling wheat in the past, are located on a hill overlooking the town and offer panoramic views of the island and the Aegean Sea. Visitors can climb to the top of the windmills for a breathtaking view of Mykonos and the surrounding area.

The Church of Paraportiani:

The Church of Paraportiani is one of the most unique and beautiful churches in Greece, located in the heart of Mykonos town. The church is made up of five small churches that have been combined into one and is a popular attraction for visitors to the island. Visitors can take a guided tour of the church to learn about its history and admire its stunning architecture.

Delos:

Delos is a small island located near Mykonos and is a UNESCO World Heritage Site. The island was once the religious and cultural center of the Aegean and is home to many ancient ruins and monuments. Visitors can take a boat tour to Delos and explore the island's ancient ruins, including the Temple of Apollo and the Terrace of the Lions.

Paradise Beach:

Paradise Beach is one of the most popular and beautiful beaches in Mykonos, located on the south side of the island. The beach is known for its clear blue waters, soft sand, and vibrant atmosphere, making it a must-visit attraction for travelers to Mykonos. Visitors can spend a day relaxing on the beach or take part in various water sports and activities.

Mykonos Town:

Mykonos Town is the capital of the island and is home to many of its famous landmarks and attractions. Visitors can wander through the narrow, winding streets and explore the town's famous churches, museums, and tavernas. The town is also a great place for shopping, with a variety of boutiques and shops selling local products and souvenirs.

Psarou Beach:

Psarou Beach is one of the most exclusive and beautiful beaches in Mykonos, located on the southeast side of the island. The beach is known for its crystal-clear waters, soft sand, and lively atmosphere, making it a must-visit attraction for travelers to Mykonos. Visitors can spend a day relaxing on the beach or take part in various water sports and activities.

Chapter 11

Outdoor activities and adventure

Mykonos is a popular destination for outdoor activities and adventure, known for its stunning natural beauty, vibrant culture, and rich history. The island is located in the Aegean Sea, near the coast of Greece, and is renowned for its pristine beaches, rolling hills, and crystal-clear waters. Whether you are a seasoned adventurer or just looking to try something new, Mykonos has plenty of options for everyone.

Hiking and Walking Tours:
Mykonos offers several scenic hiking trails that showcase its rugged terrain, stunning views of the Aegean Sea, and charming

villages. One of the most popular hikes is the trail to Little Venice, a neighborhood famous for its vibrant nightlife and beautiful sunsets. The trail offers panoramic views of the town and the sea and is a great way to experience the beauty of the island. Another popular hike is the trail to the famous windmills, located on a hill overlooking Chora (the main town).

Water Sports:

Mykonos is surrounded by crystal clear waters, making it a perfect destination for water sports enthusiasts. Visitors can go snorkeling, diving, and windsurfing to discover the island's rich marine life and stunning underwater landscapes. The popular beaches of Platis Gialos and Paradise Beach offer excellent opportunities for water sports, and rental equipment is widely available.

Boat Tours:

Mykonos is located in close proximity to several other famous Greek islands, including Delos and Rhenia, and a boat tour is an excellent way to experience these islands and the Aegean Sea. Visitors can choose from a variety of boat tours, including day trips, sunset cruises, and private charters, and enjoy the stunning scenery, swim in secluded coves, and discover hidden beaches.

Horseback Riding:

For a unique and memorable experience, visitors can explore the island on horseback. Several stables offer guided tours through the hills, valleys, and beaches of Mykonos. The tours are suitable for riders of all levels and offer a chance to escape the crowds and experience the island's natural beauty.

Paragliding:
For a truly breathtaking experience, visitors can go paragliding over the Aegean Sea and the island of Mykonos. This adventure offers stunning views of the island and its famous landmarks, including the iconic windmills, and is an unforgettable experience for thrill-seekers.

In conclusion, Mykonos offers a wealth of outdoor activities and adventures for visitors to experience. From scenic hikes and water sports to boat tours and horseback riding, there is something for everyone to enjoy on this stunning Greek island.

Chapter 12

Food and beverages

Mykonos is known for its delicious cuisine, influenced by the island's rich history and geography. Whether you're a foodie or just looking for a tasty treat, there is something for everyone in Mykonos. Here are some of the foods and beverages that you should try during your visit to the island.

Seafood:
Mykonos is surrounded by the Aegean Sea, which provides an abundance of fresh seafood. Visitors should try traditional Greek dishes like grilled octopus, squid, and sardines, as well as more elaborate seafood dishes like bouillabaisse, a fish stew made with a variety of seafood and vegetables. Many restaurants on the island serve

seafood dishes with a local twist, so be sure to ask the chef for recommendations.

Traditional Greek dishes:
Mykonos is known for its traditional Greek cuisine, and visitors should take advantage of this opportunity to try classic dishes like moussaka, a layered casserole made with eggplant, ground beef, and béchamel sauce, and tzatziki, a creamy yogurt dip made with garlic, cucumber, and olive oil. Another popular dish is Greek salad, a fresh and flavorful mix of tomatoes, cucumbers, onions, and feta cheese.

Local sweets and pastries:
Mykonos is famous for its sweets and pastries, and visitors should not miss the chance to try some of the island's famous desserts. Try loukoumades, deep-fried dough balls drizzled with honey and sprinkled with cinnamon, and baklava, a sweet pastry made with phyllo dough, honey, and chopped nuts. Other local sweets

to try include kataifi, a dessert made with shredded phyllo dough and sweet syrup, and galaktoboureko, a creamy semolina pudding encased in phyllo dough.

Wine and spirits:
Mykonos is also known for its wine and spirits, and visitors should take advantage of the opportunity to try some of the island's famous beverages. Try retsina, a resin-flavored Greek wine, and ouzo, a popular anise-flavored liquor. Visitors can also try other traditional Greek spirits like tsipouro, a pomace brandy, and metaxa, a smooth brandy made with grape must and aged in oak barrels.

Mykonos offers a wealth of delicious foods and beverages for visitors to enjoy. From fresh seafood and traditional Greek dishes to local sweets and famous wines and spirits, there is something for everyone on this stunning Greek island.

be sure to try as many of these local delicacies as possible during your visit!

10 amazing meals you should eat when you go there.

Chapter 13

Shopping and souvenirs

Mykonos is a popular shopping destination, offering a wide range of products and souvenirs for visitors to take home. From high-end designer boutiques to local artisanal shops, the island has something for everyone. Here are some of the shopping and souvenir options that you should consider while on vacation in Mykonos.

Designer boutiques:

Mykonos is a hub for high-end shopping, and visitors can find a variety of designer boutiques throughout the island. The famous Chora (main town) is home to several luxury boutiques, offering clothing, jewelry, and accessories from top international brands. Visitors can also find locally-made clothing, accessories, and gifts in several other shops throughout the island.

Artisanal shops:

Mykonos is known for its traditional crafts and artisanal goods, and visitors can find a variety of locally-made products in shops throughout the island. From pottery and ceramics to jewelry and clothing, visitors can find unique and high-quality items made by local artisans. Be sure to look for the signature blue and white colors of Greek ceramics, which are a popular souvenir and a beautiful addition to any home.

Marketplaces:

Mykonos is also home to several local markets and bazaars, offering a variety of products and souvenirs. Visitors can find everything from local cheeses, honey, and olive oil to handmade crafts, jewelry, and clothing. The markets are a great place to find unique and affordable souvenirs and gifts, and they are a fun and lively place to spend an afternoon.

Leather goods:

Mykonos is known for its high-quality leather goods, including shoes, bags, and accessories. Visitors can find a variety of local shops selling handmade leather products, many of which are of exceptional quality. These products make great souvenirs and gifts and are a unique way to remember your visit to the island.

Chapter 14

Cultural encounters and events

Mykonos is a beautiful and culturally rich island that offers visitors a wealth of opportunities to experience its rich heritage and traditions. Whether you are interested in film, music, history, or just soaking up the local culture, Mykonos is a destination that will not disappoint.

Visitors to the island will not only enjoy the beautiful landscapes and stunning sunsets, but they will also have the opportunity to participate in a number of cultural events and encounters that showcase the unique history and traditions of Mykonos.

One of the most important cultural events in Mykonos is the annual Mykonos International Film Festival. Held every summer, this festival showcases a diverse range of films from around the world and provides a platform for emerging and established filmmakers to showcase their work. The festival also includes a number of events and workshops aimed at promoting the art of filmmaking and encouraging young filmmakers.

Another cultural event in Mykonos is the annual Aegean Blues Festival. Held every July, this festival celebrates the rich history of blues music and features performances by both local and international artists. The festival attracts music lovers from all over the world and is a must-visit for anyone who loves blues music.

For those interested in the history and cultural heritage of Mykonos, the island offers a number of interesting cultural encounters. Visitors can visit the Mykonos Folklore Museum, which showcases the history and traditions of the island, including its rich maritime heritage, local customs, and traditional costumes.

The Mykonos Old Town is also a must-visit for those interested in the history and culture of the island. This charming, maze-like town is filled with narrow streets, beautiful white-washed buildings, and quaint shops and cafes. Visitors can explore the town on foot, discovering its many hidden alleys, squares, and churches, or they can take a guided tour and learn more about the history and traditions of Mykonos.

Another interesting cultural encounter in Mykonos is a visit to the island's numerous churches and monasteries. Some of the most notable include the Panayia Paraportiani, a beautiful church built in the 15th century, and the Monastery of the Dormition of the Virgin, which was founded in the 17th century and is home to a number of important religious artifacts.

Chapter 15

Respect for religion and culture

Respecting the local religion and culture is an important aspect of travel. Visitors to Mykonos should be mindful of the customs and traditions of the island and act in a manner that is respectful and considerate. By doing so, they can have a truly memorable and enjoyable experience on this beautiful Greek island.

It is important for visitors to respect the local religion and culture.

The majority of the residents in Mykonos are Greek Orthodox Christians. There are several churches on the island, including the church of Panagia Paraportiani, which is one of the most famous landmarks in Mykonos. Visitors should dress modestly when visiting these religious sites and be respectful during services.

Chapter 16

Culture in Mykonos

Mykonos has a rich cultural heritage, including traditional music, dance, and cuisine. Visitors should be mindful of cultural norms and customs, such as removing shoes before entering a home and using the right hand when eating. It is also important to avoid causing offense by using inappropriate language or gestures.

Respect for the Environment
Mykonos is known for its stunning natural beauty, and visitors should take care to respect the environment. This includes avoiding littering and respecting wildlife, such as the loggerhead sea turtles that nest on the island's beaches.

Chapter 17

Staying healthy and safe

Staying healthy and safe while on vacation is essential for a great time. By following these tips, you can have a wonderful experience in Mykonos while also taking care of your health and safety.
Visiting a new place can be exciting, but it's also important to stay healthy and safe while on vacation. Here are some tips for staying healthy and safe while visiting Mykonos.

Hydration: Mykonos can get hot and sunny, so it's important to stay hydrated. Drink plenty of water, and avoid drinking alcohol and caffeine, which can dehydrate you.

Sun Safety: The sun in Mykonos can be intense, so it's important to protect your skin. Wear sunscreen with a high SPF, wear a hat, and cover up with light clothing.

Food Safety: Mykonos is famous for its delicious seafood, but it's important to make sure it's cooked properly and free from harmful bacteria. Stick to reputable restaurants, and avoid street vendors selling unrefrigerated food.

Mosquito-Borne Illnesses: Mykonos has a number of mosquito-borne illnesses, including dengue and chikungunya. Protect yourself by using insect repellent and wearing long-sleeved clothing.

Personal Safety: Mykonos is generally a safe place, but it's still important to take precautions to protect yourself. Avoid walking alone at night, and keep your valuables safe and secure.

Water Safety: The beaches in Mykonos are beautiful, but it's important to be aware of the risks. Don't swim alone, and be mindful of strong currents and undertows.

Traffic Safety: Mykonos has narrow streets, and the traffic can be heavy. Be aware of the traffic when crossing the street, and always use crosswalks.

Making the most of your vacation.

with its beautiful scenery, exciting activities, and rich cultural heritage, Mykonos is the ultimate vacation destination. Take advantage of all it has to offer and make the most of your time on this amazing island.

Here are some tips for making the most of your Mykonos vacation.

Explore the island on foot or by scooter: Mykonos is a small island, making it easy to explore on foot or by scooter. Rent a scooter and hit the roads to see the island's stunning beaches and charming villages. Alternatively, pack a picnic and go for a hike in the hills for breathtaking views of the Aegean Sea.

Visit the famous beaches: Mykonos is famous for its crystal clear waters and pristine beaches. Some of the most popular beaches include Paradise Beach, Super Paradise Beach, and Elia Beach. Be sure to try out some water sports, such as windsurfing or kitesurfing, while you're there.

Experience the nightlife: Mykonos is known for its legendary nightlife, and there is no shortage of bars, clubs, and restaurants to choose from. For a unique experience, check out a beach club like Nammos or Scorpios. Alternatively, hit up the bars in Little Venice for a more laid-back vibe.

Visit the island's cultural sites: Mykonos is rich in history and culture, and there are several must-see sites to explore. Visit the windmills on the hill overlooking Chora, the island's main town, or take a trip to the ancient island of Delos to see the ruins of the sanctuary of Apollo.

Shop for souvenirs: Mykonos is a shopper's paradise, and you'll find plenty of unique, locally made souvenirs to bring home. Check out the boutiques in Chora for handmade jewelry, pottery, and clothing, or visit the local markets for some traditional Greek treats.

Conclusion

In conclusion, Mykonos remains one of the top tourist destinations in Greece, attracting visitors from all over the world with its unique blend of beauty, culture, and excitement. This travel guide has provided an in-depth look at the island, covering everything from its stunning beaches and iconic windmills, to its bustling nightlife and delicious cuisine.

Whether you are a first-time visitor or a seasoned traveler, Mykonos offers something for everyone. The island's picturesque streets and charming villages are perfect for those who want to soak up the local culture, while its world-famous beach clubs and lively bars cater to those seeking a more upbeat experience.

The food in Mykonos is also not to be missed. From fresh seafood to traditional Greek dishes, the cuisine on the island is as diverse as it is delicious. Whether dining at a local taverna or trying a new restaurant, visitors are sure to enjoy the island's rich culinary offerings.

In conclusion, this travel guide has aimed to provide a comprehensive look at Mykonos and what it has to offer. Whether you are planning a romantic getaway, a family vacation, or a trip with friends, Mykonos is sure to provide a memorable experience that will last a lifetime. We hope this guide has been helpful in planning your trip and we wish you a wonderful time on the beautiful island of Mykonos!

Recap of key points

Final counsel and recommendations

As you plan your trip to Mykonos, here are some final counsel and recommendations to make the most of your vacation on this beautiful Greek island.

Plan ahead: Mykonos is a popular tourist destination, so be sure to book your accommodations and activities in advance to avoid disappointment.

Get off the beaten path: While the popular beaches and bars are a must-see, try to venture out and explore the less touristy parts of the island for a more authentic experience.

Respect the culture: Mykonos is a Greek island with a rich cultural heritage, so be respectful of the local customs and traditions.

Bring appropriate clothing: While Mykonos is known for its party scene, be sure to pack appropriate clothing for visits to religious sites and more traditional villages.

Try the local cuisine: Mykonos is famous for its fresh seafood, traditional Greek dishes, and delicious street food. Don't miss the opportunity to try the local cuisine.

Rent a scooter or ATV: Renting a scooter or ATV is a fun and convenient way to explore the island and reach the more remote beaches.

Don't forget to relax: While there is plenty to see and do in Mykonos, be sure to take some time to relax and soak up the sun on one of the island's many beautiful beaches.

A vacation in Mykonos promises to be an unforgettable experience. With its stunning beauty, rich cultural heritage, and vibrant nightlife, this Greek island has something for everyone. By following these recommendations, you will be able to make the most of your time on this amazing island. Happy travels!

Printed in Great Britain
by Amazon

18327184R00051